# GROWTH

When Success, Heart, and Mind Find Alignment
Marvin Simpson

"Write the vision and make it plain."

— Habakkuk 2:2

# Dedication

To my brothers - Marlon, Duwayne, and Carlington - for walking beside me in every season.
To my parents - for their sacrifices, their strength, and their unwavering belief.
And in loving memory of my brother Wayne - whose belief in me still fuels my growth. Your voice still echoes.

# In Loving Memory of Wayne

*Wayne and me, in the early days of building a life in America.*

# Author's Note

This book is not theory. It is reflection.

It is the honest account of how success, heart, and mind did not always align in my life - and how I learned to bring them together.

Growth begins when we stop pretending we are further along than we are.

# Table of Contents

# Chapter One



*Success: The Voice of the World*

Imagine a farmer standing in a field just before sunrise.

The air is cool and still. A faint layer of morning mist hangs above the ground, and the first light of the day begins to stretch across the horizon.

He stands quietly for a moment, looking over the land.

The soil beneath his boots is soft from the night's moisture. The scent of earth rises gently in the morning air. In the distance, the quiet sounds of the waking countryside begin to stir.

Rows of soil wait patiently beneath his feet.

Nothing has grown yet.

The field looks almost empty.

But the farmer knows what others might not see.

Beneath that soil are seeds.

Seeds that will take time to grow.

Seeds that must be planted, watered, protected, and trusted long before anyone can see the result.

The farmer cannot rush the harvest.

He cannot demand the crops appear overnight.

All he can do is show up each day and do the work that growth requires.

Plant.

Tend.

Wait.

There are no guarantees in that field. The weather may turn. The market may shift. Some seasons may produce less than others.

And still, he works.

Because growth has always required patience.

Most of us learn that lesson much later in life.

That quiet discipline in the field reflects something many of us eventually come to understand:

Growth rarely happens all at once.

It develops slowly, often long before anyone notices the result.

In many ways, growth in our own lives works the same way.

We plant effort.

We nurture discipline.

And we wait.

Not always knowing when the results will appear.

Success is often the first voice we hear.

From a young age, the world begins defining what success should look like. Good grades. Recognition. Promotions. Achievement. These expectations quietly shape the way we measure progress long before we truly understand ourselves.

For many years I believed success meant reaching the next milestone as quickly as possible.

Work harder.
Achieve more.
Keep moving forward.

But over time I began to realize something important.

Success alone does not guarantee fulfillment.

You can achieve.

You can advance.

You can be recognized.

And still feel unsettled.

Growth begins when we start asking deeper questions.

Questions about purpose.

Questions about discipline.

Questions about whether the path we are following truly aligns with who we are becoming.

Looking back now, I see that growth rarely begins with confidence.

More often, it begins with discomfort.

For me, some of the earliest lessons came from a place many people would not expect.

They came from fear.

**Reflection**

Pause for a moment.

What definition of success shaped your early ambitions?

Was it recognition, achievement, or the expectation to move forward quickly?

Consider the voices that influenced how you measured progress.

Sometimes the first step toward meaningful growth is recognizing the expectations we inherited.

Now ask yourself:

What does success mean to me today?

Because real growth begins when success, heart, and mind start moving in the same direction

# Chapter Two

## *The Quiet Battle*

There was one fear that followed me through much of my early life.

It wasn't loud.

It wasn't obvious to most people.

But it was always there.

The fear of being called to the board.

Classrooms have their own rhythm. Chairs scrape across the floor. Papers shuffle. Someone taps a pencil while waiting for the teacher to continue.

Most days I sat quietly in the middle rows.

Not too close to the front.

Not too far in the back.

If the teacher's eyes moved across the room and paused near me, my body reacted before my mind did.

My chest tightened.

My hands felt heavier.

Walking to the front of the classroom felt longer than it should have.

The chalk would sit in my hand while I focused on the word written on the board.

For most students, spelling meant sounding the word out.

Break it down.
Say it slowly.
Write it.

But when pronunciation itself requires effort, that process becomes complicated.

So I learned another way.

I memorized words.

Instead of sounding them out, I stored them in my mind and repeated them until they felt familiar.

But memorization has limits.

Sometimes the pressure of the moment interrupts the memory.

And when that happened, the pause felt endless.

Not because anyone said anything directly.

But because silence in a classroom has its own language.

A whisper.

Someone shifting in their seat.

A quiet laugh that tries to stay hidden.

Nothing dramatic.

But enough to make you aware that everyone is watching.

After moments like that, I would return to my seat quietly.

But the experience didn't end there.

It replayed.

Over and over again.

I would hear the hesitation in my voice.

See the pause in my mind.

Imagine what others might have been thinking.

The classroom moved on.

I didn't.

That is the part people rarely see about quiet struggles.

The moment passes for everyone else.

But for you, it stays.

Silence became protection.

But protection has a cost.

Every time I chose silence, I reinforced the belief that speaking carried too much risk.

Looking back now, I realize something else was happening during those years.

The same challenge that made speaking difficult was also forcing me to prepare more carefully.

If I couldn't rely on spontaneous answers, I had to study harder.

If spelling required memorization, I memorized more.

If speaking required rehearsal, I rehearsed.

What began as a coping strategy slowly became discipline.

And discipline built steadiness.

There came a moment in high school when that quiet battle was tested in a different way.

I was given the opportunity to participate in a science competition.

The project excited me.

But presenting it publicly meant speaking clearly in front of judges.

My first reaction was fear.

But my brother Wayne said something simple.

"You sing in the chorus with no problem. You can do this."

He didn't dismiss the fear.

He reminded me that fear and ability can exist together.

So instead of waiting for fear to disappear, I prepared.

When the day of the competition arrived, my heart was racing.

But I had built structure.

And structure steadies fear.

When I learned that I had won gold for my project and presentation, the medal mattered.

But the realization mattered more.

Preparation did not remove fear.

It gave my mind something stronger than fear — clarity.


**Reflection**
Pause for a moment.

Think back to a time when possibility first became real for you.

Maybe it was a first job, a first opportunity, or a conversation that made the future feel closer than it had before.

Often, growth does not begin with dramatic change.

It begins quietly - with effort, belief, and the willingness to take the next step forward.

Step by step, possibility begins to take shape.

# Chapter Three

*The Voice of Logic and Survival*

I was seventeen the first time I saw snow.

Not on television.

Not in pictures.

Real snow.

It was the winter of 1996, and a blizzard had swept through New Jersey.

I stepped outside wearing a thin windbreaker - the only winter jacket I owned.

Back in Jamaica, that jacket would have been enough.

Here, it was not.

The air did not just feel cold.

It bit.

Snow covered everything.

Cars were buried beneath white drifts, sidewalks disappeared, and the wind pushed against buildings.

I stood there quietly, taking it all in.

It was beautiful.

And intimidating.

Life had changed.

I did not yet know everything this new country would require of me.

But I could already feel that survival here would demand something different.

Adaptation.

Endurance.

And the willingness to keep moving even when everything felt unfamiliar.

But inside, I was determined.

Within a month of arriving in the United States, my brother Wayne and I found our first jobs at Roy Rogers.

The restaurant was several miles from where we lived in Freehold, New Jersey.

Eventually, Wayne and I began walking home after our shifts.

Those walks became something special.

We talked about school.

We talked about the future.

Sometimes we imagined owning our own homes one day.

Other nights we talked about traveling and seeing more of the world.

One night Wayne said something that stayed with me.

"Someday we will not be walking to work," he said. "We will be driving to our own homes."

At the time, it felt like a simple dream.

But it carried belief.

Those walks were not just conversations about the future.

They were shaping the belief that our effort could eventually meet our hopes.

## The First Paycheck

Not long after we started working, we received our first paycheck.

We opened the envelope and leaned over the check together, studying it carefully.

It was not about the amount.

It was about what it represented.

It meant we had earned something in this new country.

It meant we had taken one small step forward.

It meant possibility was no longer only something we talked about.

We showed it to our mom right away.

Her first instinct was practical.

"Why don't you open a bank account?"

Instead, we held onto that check for nearly two weeks.

We would take it out and look at it again.

This is ours.

Looking back now, those early months shaped something deeper than ambition.

They built resilience.

They built gratitude.

And they taught us that the future we imagined would not appear overnight.

It would be built the same way those long walks were taken.

One steady step at a time.


**Reflection**

Pause for a moment.

Think back to a time when possibility first became real for you.

Maybe it was a first job, a first opportunity, or a conversation that made the future feel closer than it had before.

Often, growth does not begin with dramatic change.

It begins quietly - with effort, belief, and the willingness to take the next step forward.

Step by step, possibility begins to take shape.

# Chapter Four

### *Learning to Think Differently*

Opportunity rarely arrives all at once.

More often, it appears as a series of decisions that slowly change the direction of our lives.

For me, one of those decisions began with education.

After completing my associate degree in Civil Engineering Technology at Ocean County College, I transferred to Drexel University to continue my studies.

By that time I had already learned something important about growth.

Progress rarely happens in ideal conditions.

More often it happens in the middle of competing responsibilities.

Work during the day.

Classes at night.

Assignments after midnight.

That rhythm became my routine.

During the day I worked on construction projects.

In the evening I attended classes.

When the city began to quiet down, I opened my books again and continued studying.

Many of the students in the evening program were professionals balancing similar responsibilities.

You could see the fatigue in the room.

But you could also see determination.

Everyone there had made the same decision.

Keep moving forward.

Some nights the lectures stretched long. By the time I returned home, the next day was already approaching.

Assignments still needed to be completed.

Papers still needed to be written.

Sleep came later.

Balancing work and school was demanding.

But discipline rarely develops in comfort.

Those years forced me to become more intentional with my time and more focused in my thinking.

And something else began to change.

While studying engineering concepts, I discovered that I was drawn more toward construction management.

Engineering explained how structures should work.

Construction showed how those ideas became reality.

Plans turned into buildings.

Designs became something people could see and touch.

That transition fascinated me.

Eventually I made a decision that would shape my career.

I changed my major to Construction Management.

At the time it felt like a practical adjustment.

Looking back now, it was another step toward alignment.

**Reflection**

Pause for a moment.

Consider a time when you had to balance multiple responsibilities at once.

What did that season require from you?

Discipline?

Sacrifice?

Focus?

Sometimes the periods that demand the most effort also shape the skills we rely on later in life.

Growth often develops quietly in those moments.

# Chapter Five

*Service Shapes the Heart*

Not every lesson about leadership comes from work or school.

Some come from service.

Around the time my professional responsibilities were increasing, I began volunteering as an Emergency Medical Technician.

At first, the commitment seemed simple.

Serve the community.

Help people in need.

But the reality of the work revealed something deeper.

Emergency calls arrive without warning.

The radio crackles with an address.

Within moments the team is moving.

Lights flash.

Sirens cut through the quiet streets.

Every call carries uncertainty.

Sometimes the situation is minor.

Other times the circumstances are far more serious.

In those moments, responsibility becomes immediate.

You can see it in the faces of family members waiting for help.

You can hear it in the urgency of their voices.

And you can feel the weight of knowing that your actions matter.

One call early in my time on the squad changed my perspective.

It was my first call.

At the time, I did not fully understand what we were walking into.

A young family had discovered that their newborn baby was not breathing.

When we entered the home, the room felt unusually quiet.

Hope and fear were both present.

We began doing everything we were trained to do.

Airway.

Breathing.

Compressions.

Despite every effort, the outcome was not what anyone hoped for.

After the call ended, I sat in my car for a while before driving home.

Not overwhelmed.

Not dramatic.

Just still.

That moment reminded me of something important.

Leadership does not guarantee outcomes.

You can be prepared.

You can be calm.

You can follow every step correctly.

And still face situations that do not resolve the way you hope.

That experience did not harden me.

It grounded me.

Over the next nine years, I continued serving as an EMT.

Through those years, I learned something that would later shape my leadership style.

When people are afraid, they look for steadiness.

Not volume.

Not intensity.

Steadiness.

Lowering your voice.

Making eye contact.

Speaking calmly when others feel overwhelmed.

Those small behaviors build trust.

And trust creates clarity.

Service taught me that leadership often begins with presence.

With listening.

With helping others feel steady in moments of uncertainty.

Service taught me how to stay steady when outcomes were uncertain.

The next lesson was learning where that steadiness belonged.

**Reflection**

Pause for a moment.

Think about a time when someone needed your help.

Not because you had all the answers, but because you were present.

Service often reveals strengths we did not know we possessed.

Patience.

Empathy.

Composure.

Sometimes the most important leadership lessons come from simply showing up.

# Chapter Six

*When Alignment Begins*

Alignment rarely begins with certainty.

Sometimes it begins with discomfort.

There was a season in my career when, on paper, everything looked strong.

Projects were moving.

Clients were satisfied.

Responsibilities were increasing.

But inwardly, something felt still.

I remember sitting at my desk one afternoon reviewing the work in front of me.

The projects were progressing.

The feedback had been positive.

By most measures, things were going well.

Yet I could not ignore the quiet tension I felt.

Something was not moving.

Promotions were happening around me, but not for me.

At first, I dismissed the thought.

Maybe the timing simply was not right.

Maybe I needed to be patient.

Maybe the opportunity would come later.

But as time passed, the feeling became harder to ignore.

I began asking myself difficult questions.

What am I missing?

Is there something I need to improve?

Am I approaching my work the right way?

The emotion I felt most strongly during that season was not anger.

It was anxiety.

I had always believed that preparation and discipline would naturally lead to progress.

So I responded the only way I knew how.

I leaned in harder.

I reviewed my work more carefully.

I examined my communication, my writing, and the way I presented ideas.

If there was a weakness I could improve, I worked on it.

But despite those efforts, the sense of being stalled remained.

That realization was difficult for me.

Because discipline had carried me through so many earlier seasons of growth.

It helped me prepare when fear tried to silence me.

It helped me adapt to a new country and new expectations.

It helped me balance work, school, and responsibility.

It helped me stay steady in seasons that required endurance.

So naturally, I trusted discipline again.

If something felt uncertain, I worked harder.

If something felt weak, I prepared more.

If progress slowed, I tightened everything I could control.

But growth was teaching me a new lesson.

Hard work and forward movement are not always the same thing.

That lesson was uncomfortable.

When effort has been your strategy for survival and growth, it is difficult to imagine that effort may not be the issue.

Eventually, I realized something else.

I had been trying to solve the problem alone.

So I did something that did not come naturally to me.

I asked for counsel.

That decision mattered.

Not because I lacked discipline.

But because discipline and perspective are not the same thing.

The conversation began simply.

A senior leader asked about the project, how things were progressing, and the challenges we were facing.

Eventually, I shared what had been on my mind.

"I feel like I am doing strong work," I said, "but I am not moving forward the way I expected."

He did not rush to give advice.

Instead, he asked questions.

Questions about positioning.

Questions about how my work was being perceived.

Questions that helped me step back and see the situation differently.

Then he offered a simple suggestion.

What about exploring another business unit?

At first, the idea felt uncomfortable.

I had become familiar with my environment.

I knew the team.

I knew the expectations.

Leaving meant uncertainty.

But as we continued talking, something became clear.

The problem was not effort.

It was direction.

That sentence stayed with me.

Because it changed the way I understood growth.

Until then, I had measured progress mostly by output.

Work harder.

Improve more.

Stay ready.

Keep going.

But alignment asks a deeper question.

Not only, Am I giving my best?

But also, Am I giving my best in the right place?

Sometimes growth requires more than discipline.

Sometimes it requires a new environment.

A clearer perspective.

A better question.

That realization did not solve everything overnight.

There were still decisions ahead.

There was still uncertainty.

There was still risk.

But something important had begun.

For the first time, I was no longer treating effort as the only answer.

I was beginning to understand that success, heart, and mind cannot remain separated forever.

Success had taught me to pursue excellence.

Discipline had taught me to endure.

Service had taught me to remain present for others.

Now a new lesson was emerging:

Those strengths matter most when they move in the same direction.

That is what alignment began to mean to me.

Not perfection.

Not instant progress.

Not a life free from uncertainty.

Alignment begins when we stop forcing movement and start seeking clarity.

It begins when we tell the truth about what we are feeling.

It begins when we become humble enough to ask for perspective.

And it begins when we recognize that harder is not always wiser.

Looking back now, that season marked an important turning point in my growth.

Not because everything changed in a moment.

But because the question changed.

I was no longer asking only,

How do I work harder?

I was beginning to ask,

Where does my effort belong?

And often, that is where alignment begins.

But clarity does not always bring immediate movement.

Sometimes the season after direction feels quieter than expected.

**Reflection**

Pause for a moment.

Think about an area of your life where your effort is strong, but your movement feels limited.

What assumption are you making about the answer?

More work?

More pressure?

More patience?

Now ask a different question.

Is the issue your discipline?

Or is it your direction?

Sometimes alignment begins not when we force more effort,

but when we gain enough clarity to move that effort in the right place.

# Chapter Seven

### *When Progress Stalls*

Progress becomes confusing when clarity has already come.

Once we see that something needs to change, we often expect movement to follow quickly.

We assume that a better direction will immediately produce visible results.

But growth does not always work that way.

There was a season after that realization when I understood more than I had before, but outwardly, very little seemed different.

I was moving.
But not visibly.

Changing direction helped me see more clearly.
It did not remove the discomfort of transition.

A new environment brings its own kind of pressure.

In my previous setting, I knew the rhythm of the work.
I knew the team.
I knew the expectations.
I understood where problems usually surfaced and how decisions were typically made.

Now I was learning again.

That kind of beginning is humbling.

There were meetings where I spoke less and listened more.
I paid attention to how people communicated.

How decisions were made.
How tension showed up in the work.
How experienced people read a situation before they responded to it.

Some days I left with more questions than answers.

I remember the feeling of carrying those questions with me at the end of the day.
Not discouragement exactly.
Not fear.
Just the quiet awareness that I was no longer operating from familiarity.

I had entered a season where growth required observation before movement.

That was harder for me than I expected.

For much of my life, progress had been connected to visible effort.
Study more.
Work more.
Prepare more.
Push harder.
Eventually the result appears.

But this season demanded something different.

Patience.
Humility.
Restraint.

It asked me to accept that learning can still be happening even when recognition has not arrived yet.

That lesson was difficult because I had quietly linked progress to evidence.

A promotion.
A title.
A visible opportunity.
Some external sign that confirmed the work was paying off.

But growth was teaching me again.

Not all meaningful progress is public.

Some of it happens in the way you learn to listen.
Some of it happens in the way you begin to read people more carefully.
Some of it happens when your confidence becomes quieter and steadier.
And some of it happens when you stop needing immediate proof that the process is working.

Looking back now, I can see that this season was not empty.

It was preparing me.

It was teaching me how to enter new responsibility without pretending I already knew everything.
It was teaching me how to slow down and understand before trying to direct.
It was teaching me that progress can be real long before it becomes visible.

That may be one of the hardest truths about growth.

Sometimes the season that feels stalled is actually the season where capacity is being built.

Roots are forming before fruit appears.
Judgment is deepening before authority expands.
Character is being strengthened before responsibility increases.

At the time, I did not yet know how important that would become.

I did not know that greater responsibility was ahead.
I did not know that people would eventually look to me for clarity.
I did not know that this quieter season was shaping the way I would lead.

I only knew that progress felt slower than I had hoped.

But slower did not mean wasted.

And it did not mean lost.

Sometimes progress stalls because growth is happening beneath the surface.
Sometimes movement is delayed because preparation is still doing its work.
Sometimes what feels like waiting is actually formation.

That is what this season became for me.

It taught me that progress is not always measured by speed.
Sometimes it is measured by readiness.

And when the next opportunity came, I began to understand that this quieter season had not been holding me back.

It had been preparing me to carry more.

**Reflection**

Pause for a moment.

Think about an area of your life where progress feels slower than you expected.

What are you using as proof that growth is happening?
A title?
Recognition?
Visible results?

Now consider another possibility.

What if this season is not empty?
What if it is developing your patience, your judgment, and your capacity for what comes next?

Not every quiet season is wasted.
Sometimes progress appears stalled because growth is happening where others cannot yet see it.

# Chapter Eight

## *The Weight of Responsibility*

After a less visible season of learning, responsibility finally arrived in visible form.  Leadership often enters that way.

Not with applause.

Not with a dramatic announcement.

Sometimes it arrives as an assignment,

a group of people,

and the expectation that you will help move the work forward.

That moment came when I stepped into my first role managing a large department on a major project.

I remember arriving early on the first day.

The trailers were still quiet.

The normal rhythm of activity had not yet begun.

For a few moments, I stood in that stillness aware of both the opportunity and the weight of it.

There was excitement.

But there was also pressure.

After a brief conversation, the director walked me over to the department I would now lead.

The team gathered.

Introductions began.

One by one, people shared their names and their roles.

When it was my turn, I kept it simple.

"Hi, I am Marvin. I am here to support the team, and I have a lot to learn from you as well."

I meant that.

Many of the people standing there had more experience than I did.

Some had been doing this work longer than I had been in the industry.

And when you step into a moment like that, you can feel the room studying you.

People want to understand what kind of leader you will be.

Will you listen?

Will you pretend?

Will you bring confusion or clarity?

Will you make their work harder or help it move?

I realized quickly that leadership in that moment was not about proving myself with words.

It was about paying attention.

So instead of beginning with instructions, I began with questions.

What are you working on?

Where are we in the schedule?

What challenges are you seeing?

Where is the pressure starting to build?

Those conversations mattered.

They helped me understand more than the tasks.

They helped me understand the people responsible for the work.

And leadership begins there.

As I reviewed the schedule and the milestones ahead, the scale of the assignment became clearer.

The project was large.

The department was large.

And the responsibility was no longer personal alone.

Other people's work, time, and trust were now connected to how well I led.

That is the weight of responsibility.

It is not simply the pressure to perform.

It is the realization that your decisions affect others.

Soon the demands increased.

The owner began asking sharper questions.

Additional milestones appeared.

Expectations rose.

What had first felt like a leadership opportunity now revealed itself as a leadership test.

In that moment, I understood something important.

Our department did not need more motion.

It needed more clarity.

People can work hard and still pull in different directions.

They can stay busy and still lose time.

They can mean well and still create confusion.

So we brought the team together and built a plan.

We made the priorities plain.

We clarified roles.

We talked through deadlines.

We identified pressure points before they became larger problems.

And as communication improved, something started to shift.

The department did not just become busier.

It became more aligned.

People understood what mattered most.

Problems were addressed earlier.

Conversations became more direct.

The work began moving with less friction.

Over time, the results became visible.

The department was recognized as one of the top-performing groups on the program.

I was grateful for that.

But recognition was not the deepest lesson.

The deeper lesson was this:

Leadership is not about becoming the loudest voice in the room.

It is about helping people see clearly enough to move together.

That season changed the way I understood responsibility.

Before then, I often thought of leadership as influence, performance, or visibility.

But that experience taught me that leadership is also stewardship.

You are entrusted with people.

With pressure.

With timing.

With uncertainty.

And your role is not to carry all the work yourself.

Your role is to help the work move with clarity.

Looking back now, that first season of major responsibility did not just teach me how to manage a department.

It taught me how to think about leadership.

Responsibility becomes lighter when clarity increases.

And often the most valuable thing a leader gives is not control.

It is direction.

Over time, I began to see that leadership is measured not only by what gets done, but by what begins to grow in other people.


**Reflection**

Pause for a moment.

Think about a responsibility you are carrying right now.

Where do people around you need more clarity?

What pressure could be reduced if direction became clearer?

Leadership often begins when you help others understand what matters most and move together.

# Chapter Nine

### *Leadership Multiplies*

One of the most meaningful moments in leadership happen quietly.

They do not always happen in meetings.

They do not always happen in public.

And they are not always attached to titles, recognition, or visible achievement.

Sometimes they happen in conversation.

I was walking a project with a younger professional I had worked with on several assignments.

Like many of our conversations, we were reviewing the work in front of us and discussing what needed attention next.

There was nothing unusual about the moment at first.

We talked through the project.

We looked at what was moving well and what still needed clarity.

We discussed the next phase of the work, the pressure points ahead, and the decisions that would matter most.

Then the conversation shifted.

They paused and said something I did not expect.

Some of the conversations we had over the years had helped shape the way they approached their work.

The questions I asked had helped them see situations more clearly.

For a moment, I did not respond.

I was surprised.

And humbled.

Because when you are doing the work every day - solving problems, answering questions, moving from one responsibility to the next - you do not always realize what is staying with other people.

You think you are simply helping in the moment.

You think you are offering a thought, a question, a little perspective.

You do not always see the longer reach of those small exchanges.

But standing there, listening, something came into focus for me.

Leadership influence spreads quietly.

That moment mattered to me because it revealed something deeper than professional progress.

The counsel that once steadied me had not ended with me.

Earlier in my own journey, I had needed people who could help me think more clearly.

I needed people who asked better questions, offered perspective, and helped me see what I could not yet see on my own.

At the time, those moments felt personal.

They felt like help.

They felt like guidance I needed in order to move forward.

But over time, I began to understand something larger.

What is given to us in one season is often meant to be shared in another.

The clarity that strengthens us is not only for our own advancement.

It also prepares us to strengthen others.

That is one of the deepest ways leadership grows.

At first, leadership can feel connected to performance.

Can I do the work well?

Can I handle the pressure?

Can I carry responsibility?

Can I help the team move forward?

Those questions matter.

But eventually leadership becomes larger than execution.

It becomes about development.

It becomes about whether your presence helps other people grow in confidence, judgment, and clarity.

It becomes about whether your words create steadiness in someone else.

It becomes about whether your leadership stops with you or continues through the people around you.

That is why this moment stayed with me.

Because it reminded me that influence is not always dramatic.

Often it looks like a conversation.

A question asked at the right time.

A calm perspective in a pressured moment.

A small act of guidance that helps someone think differently about their work, their decisions, or their ability.

And when that person begins to offer the same kind of clarity to others, something powerful happens.

Leadership multiplies.

Its impact moves beyond a single project.

Beyond a single interaction.

Beyond a single season.

What began as counsel becomes capacity.

What began as support becomes strength.

What began as one person helping another see clearly becomes a pattern that continues.

That changed how I thought about success.

Success is not only about what you build.

It is also about what continues to grow in others because of how you led.

That kind of influence is easy to overlook because it is rarely announced.

It does not always come with visible recognition.

Sometimes you only see it years later, in a sentence, a decision, or a quiet conversation that reveals your leadership reached further than you knew.

Looking back now, I believe that is one of the most meaningful parts of growth.

Not simply becoming stronger yourself.

But becoming someone whose clarity helps strengthen others.

That is when leadership begins to multiply.

Looking back, I can see that all of these lessons were part of one larger formation.

**Reflection**

Pause for a moment.

Think about someone who influenced your growth earlier in your life or career.

What did they do that helped you see more clearly?

Did they give answers right away, or did they ask questions that helped you think differently?

Did they make you feel pressured, or did they make you feel steadier?

Now ask yourself another question.

Who around you might need that same kind of guidance from you?

Leadership multiplies when clarity is shared.

And often the influence that lasts longest begins in ordinary conversations.

# Chapter Ten

### *Steady Growth*

L ooking back, growth rarely happened the way I expected.

We imagine one decision, one opportunity, one breakthrough that suddenly changes everything.

But most of my growth did not happen that way.

It came through smaller moments.

Through repeated effort.

Through quiet correction.

Through seasons that did not feel important at the time, but later revealed how much they had shaped me.

Some of those seasons taught me discipline.

Some taught me endurance.

Some taught me how to serve.

Some taught me how to ask better questions.

And some taught me that effort alone is not enough if your direction is unclear.

At the time, those lessons felt separate.

A classroom.

A move to a new country.

A first paycheck.

Night classes after work.

Moments of service as an EMT.

Conversations with mentors.

Responsibility on a project.

Quiet conversations that later shaped someone else.

But looking back, I can see that they were all part of the same formation.

Growth was teaching me, little by little, how to bring my mind, my heart, and my pursuit of success into alignment.

That did not happen quickly.

And it did not happen in a straight line.

There were seasons when I felt uncertain.

Seasons when I felt behind.

Seasons when I had to work without immediate recognition.

Seasons when I had to accept that clarity mattered more than speed.

At times, I wanted progress to feel obvious.

I wanted visible movement.

I wanted some clear sign that everything I was learning was leading somewhere.

But growth often works more quietly than that.

It forms us before it reveals itself.

It deepens judgment before it expands responsibility.

It teaches patience before it produces confidence.

And many times, it asks us to keep walking before we can clearly see where the road is leading.

When I think about that now, my mind often returns to Wayne.

I still think about those long walks home after work.

Talking about school.

Talking about life.

Talking about the future as if saying it aloud might help us believe in it.

At the time, those walks seemed simple.

But they were shaping something deeper.

They were teaching me that progress does not always come in giant steps.

Sometimes it comes in conversation.

Sometimes it comes in belief.

Sometimes it comes in the decision to keep moving even when the distance ahead still feels long.

Those walks taught me something I would spend years understanding more fully:

steady steps matter.

The future Wayne and I talked about did not arrive all at once.

It was built over time.

Through effort.

Through correction.

Through sacrifice.

Through help from others.

Through lessons I did not always recognize while I was living them.

That is why I no longer think of growth as something dramatic.

Growth is often quiet.

It is often uncomfortable.

It is often slower than we would like.

But it is real.

It happens each time we choose discipline over drift.

Each time we stay teachable.

Each time we ask for guidance instead of pretending we already know.

Each time we stop measuring progress only by speed and start valuing clarity, faithfulness, and direction.

That is what steady growth has come to mean to me.

Not perfection.

Not constant visibility.

Not a life without setbacks.

Steady growth means continuing to move with honesty and intention.

It means allowing each season to teach what it came to teach.

It means trusting that small steps, taken consistently, can shape a life more deeply than dramatic moments ever could.

And if this journey has taught me anything, it is this:

You do not always need a breakthrough to keep growing.

Sometimes you only need the humility to learn,

the courage to keep going,

and the willingness to take the next faithful step.

That is how growth happened in my life.

And in many ways, that is how it still happens now.

One steady step at a time.

**Reflection**

Pause for a moment.

Look back over your own journey.

What lessons were forming in you before you had words for them?

What small, consistent steps helped shape the person you are becoming?

Who walked with you, encouraged you, or helped you keep going when the future was still unclear?

Growth is not always dramatic.

Often, it is built quietly over time.

Stay open.

Stay teachable.

Keep moving.

**One steady step at a time.**

# Epilogue

### *The Courage to Ask*

When I look back on this journey, I do not see a straight path.

I see moments.

Moments of uncertainty.
Moments of discipline.
Moments when I had to keep moving without full clarity.
And moments when someone asked a question that helped me see more clearly.

Those moments shaped my life more than I understood at the time.

Some happened in classrooms where I was learning how to move through fear.
Some happened during long walks home from work with Wayne, when the future felt distant but still possible.
Some happened on job sites where responsibility demanded steadiness.
And many happened in conversations with people who helped me see beyond my own perspective.

Looking back now, I understand something more clearly.

Growth rarely happens alone.

At some point, most of us need someone who can help us pause, think, and see differently.
Not always by giving us a perfect answer.
Sometimes by asking a better question.
Sometimes by offering calm perspective when our own thinking feels narrow.

Sometimes by believing in us before we fully believe in ourselves.

That kind of help matters.

It gives us courage.
It gives us room to grow.
It reminds us that uncertainty does not mean we are lost.

Over time, something changes.

The counsel we once needed becomes the counsel we can offer.
The clarity that once strengthened us becomes clarity we can share.
The questions that helped shape our lives become the questions we gently place before others.

To me, that is part of what makes growth meaningful.

It is not only that we become stronger.
It is that our growth can become a source of strength for someone else.

If this book has offered anything, I hope it has offered that reminder.

Growth does not have to be dramatic to be real.
It can be steady.
It can be quiet.
It can be formed one decision at a time.

And sometimes the step that changes more than we realize begins very simply:

with the courage to ask.

Thank you for taking this walk with me.

# Acknowledgments

No journey of growth happens alone, and this book is the result of many people who shaped my life in seen and unseen ways.

First, to my parents, thank you. Your sacrifices created opportunities that changed the course of our lives. The work you carried, often quietly and without recognition, taught me perseverance, responsibility, and faithfulness.

To my brothers — Marlon, Wayne, Duwayne, and Carlington — thank you. Growing up with you shaped who I am. The conversations we shared, the challenges we faced, and the dreams we carried together helped form the foundation of my life.

In loving memory of my brother Wayne: your belief in me never wavered. The encouragement you gave, the walks we shared, and the future we talked about still stay with me. Your life continues to shape how I think, how I lead, and how I keep moving forward.

To the mentors and leaders who offered counsel throughout my journey, thank you. Your questions, your perspective, and your willingness to guide me helped me grow in ways I could not have achieved alone.

To the teams I have had the privilege to work with and lead, thank you. Your dedication, trust, and commitment turned every challenge into an opportunity to learn, improve, and serve.

And finally, to you, the reader: thank you for taking the time to walk through these experiences with me. If any part of this book encourages you to keep growing, to stay open, and to move forward with greater clarity and purpose, then sharing it has been worthwhile.

# About the Author

Marvin Simpson is a construction professional, leader, and lifelong student of growth and alignment.

After immigrating to the United States as a teenager, he balanced work and education while pursuing degrees in engineering and construction management. Through persistence and steady effort, he built a career grounded in responsibility, service, and leadership.

Marvin also served for nearly a decade as a volunteer Emergency Medical Technician, an experience that deeply shaped his understanding of composure, service, and leadership.

Today he is passionate about mentoring others and helping professionals develop clarity, discipline, and alignment in their careers.

*Growth: When Success, Heart, and Mind Find Alignment* reflects the lessons he learned through that journey.